The Further Sayings
of Chairman Malcolm

OTHER BOOKS BY MALCOLM S. FORBES

The Forbes Scrapbook of Thoughts on the
  Business of Life
Fact and Comment
The Sayings of Chairman Malcolm
Around the World on Hot Air and Two Wheels

The Further Sayings of Chairman Malcolm

Malcolm S. Forbes

HARPER & ROW, PUBLISHERS
NEW YORK
Cambridge, Philadelphia, San Francisco, London
Mexico City, São Paulo, Singapore, Sydney

FIRST EDITION

Library of Congress Cataloging-in-Publication Data

Forbes, Malcolm S.
  The further sayings of Chairman Malcolm.

  1. Aphorisms and apothegms. I. Title.
PN6271.F58   1986   818'.5402   85-45636
ISBN 0-06-015573-6

86 87 88 89 90 KP 10 9 8 7 6 5 4 3 2 1

TO MOIRA

Whose merry love of life and people
Gives joy to the world

Contents

Foreword

Putting these Sayings to paper has been—mostly—fun. Some required more polish than others, and I'm sure you'll think some should have been polished off altogether. But they're to give you pleasure, stimulation, a chuckle or two. You may recognize old thoughts in new words or recognize some thoughts you've often had but never put in words.

Reading these Sayings isn't meant to be heavy duty. If they do put you to sleep, that could be considered a plus—sleeping pills that are non-addictive.

Enjoy! (I hope.)

Malcolm Forbes

Boardroom Banter

WHEN YOU SAY
of a potential successor, "but he's young," instead of, "good, he's young," your departure needs hastening.

HE WHO HAS THE WHEEL
determines the direction.

DEFINITION OF A VICE CHAIRMAN
Anybody (except a furniture salesman) who can sell or buy Dinner tables at $1,000 & Up (& Up & Up) for a Cause.

YOUR OWN BUSINESS
Start small and grow big.
Start big and go broke.

IF YOU DON'T ENJOY THE CLIMB
    giving what it takes to get to the top isn't worth
    it.

AN INDISPENSABLE MAN
    should be dispensed with as promptly as possi-
    ble.

THERE ARE MORE ACTORS
    in the business of business than in the profession
    of acting.

IN MANAGEMENT, THE STAID
    seldom stay long.

BOARDS
    can no longer afford bores.

CORPORATE CHIEFTAINS
    usually last less long than political potentates.

FAT
    corporate or personal, is something to get rid of.

WEIGHT
> People who carry real weight seldom throw it around. (And fat men can't seem to throw it away.)

VANITY INSPIRES
> the best acting in executive suites as well as on stage.

THE MORE WEIGHT ONE CARRIES
> the heavier the burden.

IT'S MANAGEMENT'S FAULT
> when employee turnover is high.

ANY CEO WHO CAN'T HANDLE
> down periods won't have too many years Up.

ONLY GOD IS IN A POSITION
> to look down on anyone.

THERE'S NOTHING THAT DOESN'T WORK
> until you try it.

IT'S MORE FUN
   calling the tune than importuning.

STOPPING IN TIME
   is more important than arriving on time.

IF YOU'VE NEVER BEEN DOWN
   how would you know what up is?

ATTENTION IS TO PEOPLE
   what fertilizer is to flowers.

Bottom Line

A DRIP

is a drain.

GIVING

Give what you want and you'll get what you give.

TASTE

In these days of revised morals and revived styles, Bad Taste is now only something that tastes bad.

A BORE

One who consistently changes his own views to conform with ours.

WHOEVER DESIGNATED SEASONS'
first days certainly knew nothing about
weather.

DISAPPOINTMENTS
most often come from unwarranted expecta-
tions.

SMOKING
Those who do, make those who don't—smoke.
Those who don't, make those who do—smoke.

ACT OF FAITH
To view the end as a beginning.

AN OCCASION
is easily created by an unexpected gesture or
deed.

INSTANT CONCLUSIONS
befit bereft minds.

SERVILITY
Antithesis of sincerity.

MACHO-DO
is usually about nothing.

SENSITIVITY
to slight lessens as life lengthens.

BEAUTIFUL PEOPLE (NÉE CAFÉ
SOCIETY, NÉE JET SET)
Those to whom visibility matters more than
their lives' viability.

LIVING
What you learn and earn from whom and what
you know.

SCHTICK
is schic.

DREAMS
as often as not are the reality.

PRESENCE IS MORE
   than just being there.

LIFE AND LIVING
   can be simple only if you are.

WISHFUL THINKING
   is a contradiction in terms.

MATTERING
   matters.

FUN
   isn't as much unless shared.

VIRTUE
   is always a relative thing.

Executive Sweets

UNLESS THEIR BIZ IS SHOW BIZ
   people who must get phone calls at their restau
   rant tables shouldn't be dining publicly.

A SHARP KNIFE
   tenderizes most any steak—as every sharp
   restaurateur knows.

TO ENJOY ANY MEAL
   be hungry.

DUCK
   Easier to shoot than cook.

MANY RESTAURANTS DO DUCK
   but in most cases the customers should.

WANNA WAIST AWAY?
Eat less.

STOMACH WHAT YOU MUST
especially good food.

CHECKING THE RESTAURANT
check reflects as much good sense as the dollars
it often saves.

RESTAURANTS THAT SERVE TOOTH-
PICKS
deserve as customers those who use 'em then
and there.

CATCHING AN EYE
in too many restaurants is as hard as it would be
literally everywhere but at a nomad sheik's ban-
quet.

SURLY WAITERS
spoil more meals than bad cooks.

SOUP'S
> better to eat than to be in.

A RESTAURANT THAT WON'T
> accept a credit card has to be really good—or awful.

FAT PEOPLE
> are said to be enjoying life—but unless they heave the heft there's probably less of it left.

THOSE WHO LIVE FOR THEIR EN-
> TRANCE
> are usually made a meal of.

A RASPBERRY
> can be either delicious or expressive.

DIET
> is not a matter of what but how much.

IF THE DINNER CHECK'S DELAYED
> try leaving.

AS ONE STRAWBERRY SAID TO THE
OTHER
"It's because we were in the same bed that we
got into this jam."

THOSE WHO LIVE TO EAT
are at least making the most of one necessity.

WHO NEEDS CHICKENS
when most of us have no trouble laying so many
eggs?

IT'S TOO BAD IRRESISTIBLE FOOD
always goes to waist.

DEFINITION OF PATHOS
Your dog watching you eat.

WATCHING YOUR DIET
is easier than following it.

"BON APPÉTIT"
is a blessing.

General Counsel

NECESSITY IS THE MOTHER
of motivation.

IT'S TOO BAD
that manners and money so seldom go hand in
hand.

THOSE WHO WON'T ASK
for advice most need it.

IF YOU'VE MADE YOUR POINT
let it go at that.

THE BEST ADVICE
Refrain from giving any.

CRITICIZING DOERS
   is far less fun than doing.

IN PEOPLE
   what you look for you find.

NEVER BE WILLING
   to adjust to failure, or you'll always be.

NEVER PERISH
   a good thought.

WASTED EXPERTISE
   Those in a position to report authoritatively on
   the next life never seem to get through to pros-
   pects.

A JOB IN HAND
   is worth a dozen in prospect.

IF YOU START OUT
   sure you won't luck out, you won't. So don't.

IF YOU REALLY CARE
others will too.

BEING THE LAST TO LEAVE
inevitably spoils what you overstayed for.

TO STICK WITH A MISTAKE
is worse than making one.

SHOWING YOUR BRIGHTNESS
is seldom illuminating.

IT'S EASIER TO GRAB SUCCESS
than to hold on to it.

MOTIVE
A man who does praiseworthy things for praise
usually doesn't get what he doesn't deserve.

THOSE WHO FEAR FAILURE
can never succeed greatly.

ALCHEMY ISN'T A MYTH
Attitude and action can turn anyone and anything golden.

THE TRIP
is a short one if you're enjoying it. If you want it to seem long, don't.

YOU'RE NEVER WRONG
to do the right thing.

IS IT WISE
to prove you're right if it proves your boss is dumb?

GIVING ADVICE
is less expensive than following it.

TO GET
ask.

NO ANSWER
is often the best answer.

TO ENJOY THE MOST
don't expect too much.

THE MOMENT YOU THINK YOU'RE
DOING
your company a favor by working for them,
quit. Before you're fired.

YOUR DEGREE OF DETERMINATION
determines your outcome.

THOSE WHO SNAP FINGERS
to get attention are seldom worth a snap of anyone else's.

NO ACTION IS
often a better reaction than precipitous action.

THE SHORT WAY
to reach an objective is often roundabout.

GOOD INTENTIONS
are no substitute for good results.

IF YOU WANT TO BE THE WHOLE DEAL
no one will want to deal with you—other than
to deal you out.

DREAMS COME TRUE
for those who tackle the nitty-gritty.

CHARGING
beats retreating.

IF YOU DON'T WANT TO
don't.

DO NOUGHT
and you'll be.

NEVER ACKNOWLEDGE
and you won't be.

TO BE SURE OF GETTING
what you want, want not.

IF YOU CAN AFFORD
   to carry your weight, you're lucky.

COMING ON STRONG
   helps when you're not.

IT'S RARELY A MISTAKE
   to give the boss credit when it isn't due.

NOBODY CAN MAKE ANYBODY
   be someone he or she doesn't want to be.

AS SOON AS SOMEONE SAYS
   "I'm only kidding," he usually isn't.

LOOK ON THE DAY AS A CHORE
   and it will be.

WAKE UP GLAD YOU CAN
   and it'll be a good day.

IF YOU HAVE NO CRITICS
   you likely have no successes.

THE HARDEST JOB IS
   no job at all.

THE HARDEST WORK
   is trying to avoid it.

FORBEARANCE ENABLES ONE
   to bear burdens better

SIMPLE SOLUTIONS
   seldom are.

BEING CONFIDENT IS GREAT
   when there is reason for it.

EVERY ONCE IN A WHILE
   it's good to remember that everything's tempo-
   ral—including bad and gloom, not just good and
   glad.

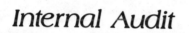

Internal Audit

IT TAKES A DIM BULB
   to shine when there's no one there to see the
   light.

ACCEPTING BLAME DUE
   before it's proffered sometimes softens the pen-
   alty.

SOLACE
   Better to lose hair than head.

BEING GOOD AND BEING ABLE
   to do good don't always go hand in hand.

IN SOME CIRCUMSTANCES, MIRAGES
   save lives that reality would lose.

YOU CAN'T FOOL
the mirror—what you see is what you are.

GIVING MAY INDEED BE MORE FUN
than getting, but you won't get if you don't have
fun at it.

FLATTERY'S HARD TO HANDLE
but most of us would like more practice.

FEIGNING
invariably fails.

ONE IS JUSTIFIED IN FEELING IN-
FERIOR
when he seeks to cover it with arrogance and in
insolence.

WHAT YOU LOOK FOR
is what you'll see.

NO ONE'S DULL WHO
shines at something.

PIECE OF MIND IS MUCH EASIER
   to give than peace of mind.

ANYONE CAN WALK ON WATER
   if it's shallow enough.

THE TEST OF FAIRNESS
   is how fair you are to those who are not.

TO DO IS FAR MORE
   than to be.

THE EFFECTS OF A MOOD
   usually outlast it.

IT'S BETTER
   to show some tension than to disguise it with
   pretension.

THE SELF-SATISFIED
   never really are.

BETTER TO BE OUT
   than never to have been In.

BEING STOIC
   about the adversities and pain of others is
   easier.

UP'S GOOD
   Uppity ain't.

PEOPLE WITH
   no problems are.

A BLEEDING HEART
   makes life more livable than a hard head.

WHERE YOU'RE GOING
   matters more than where you're at.

WHEN ONE STARTS TO THINK
   that he deserves his blessings, he doesn't.

IT'S A RARE MIRROR
that provokes reflection.

IGNORANCE RATHER THAN
INTENTION
accounts for most rudeness.

MERIT
is something we expect in others than our-
selves.

ONE WHO NEVER MAKES MISTAKES
never was . . . nor should be.

WHEELER-DEALERS
don't make mistakes of ignorance, but usually of
avarice.

THE BEST VISION
Insight.

IS THERE ANYTHING SADDER
than a laugh that's bitter?

HE WHO FINDS SELF
    endlessly fascinating is boring from within.

PEOPLE
    who can cry on cue have no emotions.

CHOICES
    To do or not to do precedes the option of to be
    or not to be.

THE MEMORY OF HAPPY MOMENTS
    is often even happier.

HEART-Y THOUGHTS
    Only the headless are heartless. Heartache en-
    larges both heart and horizon.

HEADWAY
    One way to get a head—pour it.
    A better way to get ahead—use it.

SELECTIVE RECOLLECTION
makes life possible; total recall does the opposite.

IF YOU'VE NO ONE OR NOTHING
to be anxious about, you should be.

TOUCHY PEOPLE
are seldom truly touched.

EGO MAY BE THE SPARK
but heart's the engine.

THOSE WHO DEMEAN
those who do business either cannot—or don't
need to.

WHAT'S IN A SOUL
a face reflects.

EYES OFTEN REVEAL MORE
than the tongue.

THE MORE SYMPATHY YOU GIVE
    the less you need.

THE HARDEST CANCER TO CUT OUT
    is self-sympathy.

SELF-SYMPATHY
    destructs one's self.

FOR COMPETITORS
    the audience is the adrenaline.

THOSE WHO CARE MOST
    about where It's At, seldom know where
    they're at.

HATING MAKES THE HATER
    hateful.

"In" Vestments

STOP MAKING A SPECTACLE
of yourself; if you can't see, get glasses.

PARENTS AND OFFSPRING
are usually closer in appearance than in thought.

SURFACE NEVER COVERS
lack of substance.

WHEN IT COMES TO FASHION
way out never is.

STYLE IS ONE THING
fashion usually quite another.

JEWELRY'S GREAT ON LADIES
   and grates on men.

MEN WHO WEAR JEWELS
   aren't.

ONE'S CARRIAGE
   conveys much of one's person.

MEN TO WHOM HOW THEY LOOK IS
IMPORTANT
   are more often than not unimportant.

WHY IS IT
   that girls who are not surface pretty are invariably much more beautiful in the real sense of
   that word?

STYLE
   cannot be created out of whole cloth.

LADIES WHO MAKE AN EFFORT
   to look their best, do.

42

TAKING OFF
    those who put on isn't hard.

UNLESS YOU'RE OF THE THEATER
    substance, not appearance, is what matters.

APPEARANCES
    The least shocked have to appear the most.

GOOD SOULS
    and heels are seldom joined.

A THIN SKIN
    cannot contain very much.

BLAZING SPORTSCOATS
    are for when the sun is.

ONE WHO'S THREADBARE
    bears all.

SECOND THOUGHT ON REALITY &
APPEARANCE
If you can't tell the difference, what difference
does it make?

VESTS ARE SO SILLY
unless you have a Phi Beta Kappa key.

BEING TOO FASHIONABLE
is always un.

IF THE SHOE FITS
you're lucky.

YOU CAN JUDGE A MAN A BIT
when—and if—he pulls up his socks.

IF YOU'RE TOO BIG FOR YOUR
BRITCHES
get a bigger pair.

The Learning Curve

The Learning Curve

WHETHER ONE ENDS UP A CYNIC
or a wise man depends on the seasoning added
along the way.

INTOLERABLE
Intolerance.

DULLNESS AND DUMBNESS
usually go hand in hand.

ANYTHING YOU KNOW HOW TO DO
is easy. If you don't, even the easiest isn't.

IN LIEU OF KNOWLEDGE
many affect superiority.

WHEN YOU STOP LEARNING
you're either dead or dumb.

WHO'S THE FOOL?
The fool's the one who fools himself that he's
fooling others.

ANYONE WHO DOESN'T LEARN
from defeat will never be a winner.

THOSE YOU'D THINK WOULD KNOW
are often the last to.

TO KNOW WHAT'S ENOUGH
is to know more than most.

WHEN SOMEONE THINKS
he knows it all, you know he doesn't know
enough to do the job.

POOLED JUDGMENTS
usually don't hold water.

INTERCHANGEABLE WORDS
Intolerant—ignorant.

ARROGANCE AND IGNORANCE
are one and the same.

THOSE WHO KNOW LITTLE
are wise to know those who know much.

ENLIGHTENING THE EDUCATED
is the toughest job of all.

THOSE WHO WON'T LEARN
from experience are multitudinously more than
the few who do.

EDUCATION'S PURPOSE
To replace an empty mind with an open one.

IT TAKES A DUMMY
to think smart people always are.

KNOWING ANYTHING FOR SURE
   is never possible.

A RUN-IN
   beats a run-out.

MIST
   masks reality.

RUBBING IT IN
   doesn't compare to the joy of rubbing it out.

THE QUESTION'S NOT TO BE
   or not be. It's what to be.

MUSIC MAY ''SOOTHE THE SAVAGE
   BREAST''
   but wars couldn't be fought without it.

CLASSY
   is a word that isn't.

Liquid Assets

ANTIDOTE TO/FOR WHINERS
   Wine.

TO PUT WHITE WINE AHEAD
   of red is like preferring first base to second.

READING WINE LISTS
   from right to left is common sense—and can
   save uncommon sums.

WINE AND WISDOM
   are ofttimes related.

WINE
   loosens the tongue, binds the friendship—and
   softens the bowels.

THINKING DRIVES SOME TO DRINK
  while drinking inspires some to think.

THE REASON THE ENGLISH CALL
    RED WINE
  "claret," I guess, is because if one has enough of
  it everything becomes more clarefied.

PAYING TOO MUCH
  for a bottle of wine spoils the taste.

PERRIER SALES ARE BUBBLING
  but it's flat in a mixed drink.

FOR ENHANCING ANY MEAL
  the only thing that beats good wine is a better
  one. Come to think of it, even a poor one is
  better than none at all.

IF YOU DON'T KNOW WHERE YOUR
    BREAD
  is buttered, you soon don't have any.

More or Less

THERE'S NO SUCH THING
as being Nobody or having Everything.

IT'S MORE FUN TO KNOW
a little about a lot than a lot about little.

MORE THAN ENOUGH
is too much.

IT'S SO EASY
to buy a lot and get little.

VERY OFTEN
less is more.

WHAT'S EVERYTHING?
Nothing is everything.

AMONG THE SILLIEST CLICHÉS
How can anyone be said to "have everything"
when no one knows what everything is?

THE GREATER THE EGO
the less the reason.

TOO LITTLE
usually lasts longer than too much.

THE MORE YOU EAT
the more you eat.

THESE DAYS THERE'S LESS
to be sure of but much to be positive about.

UNFORTUNATELY, WHAT WE ARE
is less often what we want to be, more often
what we appear to be.

SO LITTLE
  can reveal so much.

WITHOUT PUSH
  pull's useless.

IF THERE'S NOTHING TO LOSE
  or nothing to gain, what's the point?

NOTHING IS EVER
  like it used to be.

NEITHER
  are we.

HAVING SOMETHING AHEAD
  beats having a lot behind.

THE ONLY THING BETTER THAN
  the occasional three-day weekend is a four-day
  one.

THE LEAST FUN
  are those who think they're the most.

TWO LINES ARE HARDER TO WRITE
  than two pages.

DOING TWO THINGS AT ONCE
  Living a good life while leading the good life is
  easier claimed than accomplished.

Real Worth

TO BE FREE
    one must have "bread."

HEALTH AND WEALTH
    are most appreciated by those who don't have
    'em.

WHEN A BIG WALLET
    leads to a Big Head, the two soon sever.

WANNA WASTE MONEY?
    Buy diet books.

WANNA MAKE MONEY?
    Write one.

A FREE RIDE
  is most always the most expensive.

MONEY
  Those who devote their lives to piling it up, find
  the things they most want can't be bought.

WHEN PEOPLE HAVE SOMETHING
  to lose, they fight not to.

WHO GETS THE BEST?
  Those who don't have to worry about the price
  —or those who do?

A LITTLE MONEY PROVIDES
  a lot of independence.

DO YOU REMEMBER WAY BACK
  WHEN BANKS
  used to be criticized for being too conservative?

ONE'S REAL WORTH IS
  never a quantifiable thing.

TASTE AND COST
    are usually unrelated.

MONEY MAKES
    only a material difference.

MOST OF THE THINGS MONEY
    is the root of ain't evil.

THOSE "WELL OFF" ARE NOT
    necessarily so.

WHY IS IT THAT
    those who don't have it, show it?

SUBTRACT A PERSON'S MATERIAL
    worth and what's left is his real worth.

ANYBODY WHO THINKS MONEY
    is everything has never been sick. Or is.

HAVING PLENTY OF DOLLARS
can sometimes substitute for having little sense.

MONEY
Once people have enough of it (rare), they most want the things it can't buy.

HAVING LOTS OF CENTS
adds much to the other five.

WEALTH IS IN
the heart not in the wallet.

OCCASIONALLY INDULGING
in a do-nothing day is more than worth the price.

JUDGING FROM THEIR GURU-VY LIFESTYLES
many of our prophets are not without profit. Their success is measured more by their bottom lines than their heavenly ones.

LOVE IS FREE
but at what a price!

A GOOD DOCTOR
is beyond price. And bills accordingly.

IN LIEU OF INCOME
why not affect indifference?

OVERHEARD IN A RESTAURANT
"Do you think health and happiness can buy money?"

CREDIT IS MOST OFTEN GIVEN
when it's not claimed.

WHAT'S WRONG WITH MONEY?
Having none.

MONEY'S MERITS
are measured by its use, not amount.

MONEY SELDOM CHANGES PEOPLE
  It just makes them more visible.

WHO'S AN INTELLECTUAL?
  Anyone with genuine intelligence.

IF YOU CAN WRITE
  it doesn't matter if you're tongue-tied.

DEVOTED SERVICE
  is as rare as it is deserved.

Shop Talk

HOW CAN ANYONE "TELL ALL"
  when no one knows all.

NOT TOPPING ANOTHER'S TALE
  is what makes you a welcomed conversationalist.

CONVERSATION INTENDED
  to impress does indeed—in exactly the opposite
  way.

THOSE WHO SAY
  "What can I say?" usually then do—intermina-
  bly.

71

BEFORE YOU SAY
   what you think, be sure you have.

FOR THE ULTIMATE
   in stilted conversations, listen to former hus-
   bands and wives.

THE IDEAL CONVERSATIONALIST
   is one who listens—and agrees.

CONVERSATION
   Some say it's a dying art, with everybody in
   front of the boobtube. I don't really know if
   conversation is increasing or decreasing, but we
   have all had some where the pauses were the
   best part.

SAYING WHAT YOU THINK
   is a luxury that you can't always afford.

THOSE WHO KNOW THE MOST
   most often say the least.

ALL OF US LIKE
> to be thought agreeable, but not at the price of always agreeing.

IF YOU HAVE A MIND
> it is not always sane or safe to say what's on it.

TO SEDUCE MOST ANYONE
> ask for and listen to his opinion.

TO SAY NO
> when Yes is in order is to cause disorder.

PEOPLE MOST WORTH
> talking about often are not.

THE DIFFERENCE BETWEEN
> talking a lot and saying a lot lies in knowing what you are talking about.

SAYING NOTHING
> is sometimes the right thing to say.

NOBODY'S EVER INSULTED
   by a compliment.

CODA TO AD NAUSEAM
   "To make a long story short . . ."

A LOT OF PEOPLE HAVE TO
   open their mouths to learn what they think.

WHY DO WE ALWAYS TALK LOUDER
   when it's an overseas phone call—and pidgin
   our English when we're abroad and can't speak
   the language?

Short Takes

I HEARD A MEMBER OF THE YOUNG-
ER GENERATION

observe, "If I could remember what happened
at the party last night, I'd sure like to forget it."

ALONENESS INCREASES

as one lives on beyond the allotted span. Con-
temporaries disappear at an ever-increasing
rate and the communications gap with latter-
day generations gets harder to bridge. One sure
way to keep the visitors coming for those 85
years and up is to have their will to live accom-
panied by something to will.

IF YOU DON'T KNOW WHAT TO DO

with many of the papers piled on your desk,
stick a dozen colleagues' initials on 'em, and
pass them along. When in doubt, route.

SOLAR ECLIPSES—RARE AS RHINE-STONES

I can remember—ofttimes—as a kid, standing outdoors and holding a piece of film before my eyes to watch what, each time, was billed as a "rare" or "once in a lifetime" solar eclipse. It seems every two or three years ever since those days, there's been a similar to-do about solar eclipses. Don't you get the feeling that this repetitive solar phenomenon is about as rare as jewels at a society charity ball or rhinestones in a discotheque?

"IT'S A BIG, WIDE, WONDERFUL WORLD YOU LIVE IN"

goes the most famous line of that famous song. True, most of the time. My father used to phrase it differently when we youngsters occasionally complained about some injustice: "Son, never forget, this is a wonderful world to give in, but a terrible world to have to beg, borrow or steal in."

Sweat Equity

STAY SLIM
    and die later.

STAYING THERE
    is usually harder than getting there.

ADIDAS DON'T A RUNNER MAKE
    Only running does.

WALK NOT AND YOU'LL
    weigh up.

RUNNING
    provides no escape.

WORKING AT IT
   is the only way to make it so.

IF SOMEONE READS
   you write better.

IF SOMEONE'S WATCHING
   you play better.

IF SOMEONE BUYS
   you paint better.

IT'S AN ADULT MYTH
   that childhood is idyllic.

THE HARDEST PART OF LIFE
   is growing up.

Time Constraints

EVEN THE OLD GOATS ARE BENE-
FITING A BIT
from the greater tolerance, broader under-
standing that younger generations have
brought to the subject of sex. In the nomencla-
ture of the new morality, those who used to be
termed Dirty Old Men are now referred to as
Sexy Senior Citizens.

LIFE IS NEVER
as you used to think it was going to be.

TIME SPENT
is irreplaceable.

A CONTENTED MAN
is either over the hill or doesn't know there is one.

WHEN YOU'RE OLD ENOUGH
for no one to say not to eat all the sweets you want, you do.

APROPOS OF AGE
Chicks chirp. Hens cluck.

AS YOU GET OLDER
Don't slow down. Speed up. There's less time left.

AGE-OLD DIFFERENCE
The young always want to be older and the older always want to appear younger.

NUFF SAID
If you live long enough to know about enough, you're usually old enough no longer to care enough.

ARE YOU OLD ENOUGH TO
REMEMBER
when two bits was worth something?

ONLY WHEN WE'RE RUNNING
out of it do we truly begin valuing time.

TEMPUS
fugits, without a doubt, except when things are
difficult.

WHY DO THOSE OF US
who grow older blow harder . . . even when
we're not at a high altitude?

RETIREMENT
kills more people than old age.

THOSE WHO WANT TO HAVE SOME
FUN
out of life, do.

WHEN YOUNG, YOU'RE SHOCKED
by the number of people who turn out to have
feet of clay. Older, you're surprised by the number of people who don't.

THE GAP
To young people everything looks permanent,
established, and, in their eyes, practically everything should be, needs to be, changed. To
older people almost everything seems to
change, and in their view almost nothing
should. Anyone in doubt about the generation
gap?

ANYONE WHO HAS TO KILL TIME
is indeed bereft.

SURE SIGN OF AGE
When one's conversation is sprinkled with "remember!"

THE YOUNG
enjoy feeling their age.

THE OLD
  don't.

MAKE THE MOST
  of your short time here. Who knows if and
  what's next? Eternity, they say, is a long time.

HOW TO MAKE A GUY FEEL HIS AGE
  Read in your college class notes about mates
  who are retiring.

THE ONLY THING NEVER REPLACED
  The time of your life.

OLD AGE
  is hereditary.

ONLY WORMS HAVE ANY REASON
  to believe in human reincarnation.

IF THE MOMENT IS AT HAND
  prolonging it could lose it.

BEING YOUNG AND WILLING
certainly beats the reverse.

TO BE TOUCHING
is to be young.

AMONG THE SILLIER ADAGES
is that admonishment to "act your age." The
one has nothing to do with the other.

YOUTH IS WASTED
if you spend it getting ready to be old.

WE ARE NOT AMONG
things timeless.

IF I SHOULD DIE BEFORE I WAKE
gee, I'll really be sorry.

TO LIVE YOUR LIFE
in the fear of losing it is to lose the point of life.

THOSE WHO SPEAK OF KILLING
    TIME
    arc deadly.

COME ALIVE
    Since we cannot live forever—at least here—it's
    better to live a little while we are alive.

THE DEAD WILL ALWAYS BE WITH
    US
    so spend more time appreciating the living.

WE ALL LIVE LONG ENOUGH
    to die.

IT'S SAD
    that deserving life's goodies so often doesn't co-
    incide with receiving them.

MAYBE IT'S TRUE
    that you can't go home again, but that's no rea-
    son not to try.

TO BE BITTER
    is a waste of life that's short enough already.

TO BE GONE
    is to be dead. To be far gone is to be courting it.

WHEN YOU CATCH
    what you're after, it's gone.

LIFE'S TURNING POINT
    When first you wonder where your future has gone.

BLAMING DESTINY IS A POOR OUT
    for those who don't reach desired destination.

JUST AS NO MODE IS ENDURING
    so, too, no mood.

I'D RATHER GO DOWN IN FLAMES
    than end up in 'em.

Up the Hill

WHETHER IT'S IN BUSINESS OR THE
    POLITICAL WORLD
    those out bore those within.

WHEN IT COMES TO MASSAGING
    FIGURES
    masseurs are amateurs compared to politicono-
    mists.

TO BE ELECTIVE
    one cannot be selective.

AS MUCH AS WE BADMOUTH LEGIS-
    LATORS
    for what they do, they pretty much do what
    they think the majority of voters want them to
    do.

THERE'S A LOT TO BE SAID FOR
    THIN AIR
    Look at all the money Washington makes out of
    it.

RESULTS OFTEN FOLLOW
    when adrenalin flows.

IN POLITICS
    the bad actors put on the best act.

FORTUNATELY MOST POLITICOS
    would rather be heard than heeded.

THERE ARE MORE AND BETTER
    actors in politics than on all the legitimate
    stages put together.

IN POLITICS A HARD MAN
    is good to find.

AMBITION IS BEST
    not naked.

Who's Who

WHY IS IT SO MANY WANT
>to be what they're not while what they are is
>what others want to be?

BE YOURSELF
>When yourself is something to be—which for
>most of us is not all that often.

BEING A GENTLEMAN OR A LADY
>is much more a matter of heart than manners.

WHERE YOU'RE FROM
>only matters in relation to where you are.

THE TRULY SINGULAR ''BEAUTIFUL
PEOPLE''
>are those to whom it would never occur that
>they are.

NOBODY MATTERS
who matters to nobody.

THOSE WHO LIVE THEIR LIVES
for their entrances are seldom missed at their exit.

THOSE MOST ENTITLED TO EGO TRIPS
are the least likely to take them.

EVERYBODY THINKS ''THE PUBLIC''
is somebody else.

SHORT PEOPLE
try harder to stand tall in the world.

WHAT DOES IT MATTER TO YOU
who was at fault if you're the dead one.

A LITTLE CHICKEN MAKES A BIG LION
The only lions that get to be big lions are lions who know when to be a little chicken.

NO EXCEPTION
There are no exceptions to the rule that every-body likes to be an exception to the rules.

BIG MEN
are rarely small. And vice versa.

BOURGEOIS
Those who use the word.

SOMETIMES THE ORDINARY
is what's extraordinary.

THOSE WITH THE LEAST
sense of humor laugh loudest.

PUBLICITY
unmakes as many names as it makes.